365 Positive Affirmations for Teens to Build Confidence

A Year of Daily Inspiration and Wisdom to Help You Overcome Insecurity, Conquer Fear, Defeat Self-Doubt, and Enjoy Your Teen Life

Grace Cohen

Copyright © 2022 by Grace Cohen

All rights reserved.

The content contained within this book may not be reproduced, duplicated or transmitted without direct written permission from the author or the publisher. Under no circumstances will any blame or legal responsibility be held against the publisher, or author, for any damages, reparation, or monetary loss due to the information contained within this book. Either directly or indirectly. You are responsible for your own choices, actions, and results.

Legal Notice:

This book is copyright protected. This book is only for personal use. You cannot amend, distribute, sell, use, quote or paraphrase any part, or the content within this book, without the consent of the author or publisher.

Disclaimer Notice:

Please note the information contained within this document is for educational and entertainment purposes only. All effort has been executed to present accurate, up to date, and reliable, complete information. No warranties of any kind are declared or implied. Readers acknowledge that the author is not engaging in the rendering of legal, financial, medical or professional advice. The content within this book has been derived from various sources. Please consult a licensed professional before attempting any techniques outlined in this book. By reading this document, the reader agrees that under no circumstances is the author responsible for any losses, direct or indirect, which are incurred as a result of the use of the information contained within this document, including, but not limited to, — errors, omissions, or inaccuracies.

Contents

Social Skills For Teens With Social Anxiety	V
Introduction	1
JANUARY	5
FEBRUARY	19
MARCH	31
APRIL	43
MAY	55
JUNE	67
JULY	79
AUGUST	91
SEPTEMBER	103
OCTOBER	115
NOVEMBER	127
DECEMBER	139
Conclusion	149
Leaving a Review	151

References 153

About the Author 159

Social Skills For Teens With Social Anxiety

I have another equally interesting book "Social Skills For Teens With Social Anxiety," which is also available for purchase on Amazon.

This book provides guidance on a multitude of topics, including how to triumph in social situations, make friends effortlessly, and construct unshakeable self-confidence.

Scan the QR Code below

https://mybook.to/ss4twsa

Introduction

Being a teenager is challenging — it is characterized by a variety of ups and downs, of highs and lows. You're experiencing dramatic physical, mental, and emotional changes, all while trying to navigate friendships and family relationships along with schoolwork. On top of this, teens are also expected to learn about themselves during these formative years. With so much pressure on their shoulders, it's no wonder that many struggle with confidence and self-esteem issues.

But even while being a teenager might be tough, there are many wonderful aspects to it as well. You're at a phase of life where you're figuring out your identity, areas of interest, and the things you can be passionate about. You're discovering new things about yourself and the world around you. Additionally, you are evolving into the original and possibly best version of yourself.

No matter how stressful your life may be, there are always things you can do to maintain a positive attitude and feel good about yourself. The teenage years can be some of the happiest in your life, especially if you surround yourself with good influences and positive affirmations.

What are positive affirmations?

Positive affirmations are short, powerful statements that can help you change your negative mindset into a more positive one. If you're feeling down or stressed, repeating a positive affirmation to yourself can calm your nerves and make you feel confident about life — especially if it's something as simple as "Today is going well for me."

These positive affirmations are a good way to start your day, and they can help you stay focused on the positive things throughout your day. So, try reading through this list of positive affirmations for teens every morning, and find ones that resonate with how you feel.

How to get started?

Here is a list of 365 positive affirmations that you can use to build confidence and feel good about yourself.

Take a few minutes each day to read the designated affirmation. Repeat it out loud whenever you need to throughout the day, write it down in your journal, or post it where you'll see it frequently. In addition, you can bookmark your favorite affirmations to reread later and reflect on the impact they've had.

These affirmations serve as reminders that you are strong, capable, and deserving. But the words alone won't do anything for you. It's your actions that matter most — personalize these to fit your unique situation by claiming them every time they cross your mind.

JANUARY

January 1

I am capable of achieving anything I set my mind to.

No matter how challenging they may be, I will never give up on my goals. I keep fighting for what I want because I know I can overcome any obstacle life throws at me. I never stop having confidence in my skills and abilities.

"To be yourself in a world that is constantly trying to make you something else is the greatest accomplishment."

— Ralph Waldo Emerson

January 2

I am in control of my own happiness.

I'm not going to sit around and wait for anybody to make me happy. I take the initiative and pursue my personal happiness since I am in command of it. I live my life according to my own terms, not the way others expect me to.

January 3

I am worthy of love and respect.

I recognize that I am a unique individual with a lot to offer and thus, deserve genuine love and respect. So, no matter what anyone says or does, I will never accept anything below my worth — for I know that being treated kindly is indeed an irreplaceable right of mine.

January 4

I am comfortable in my own skin.

I'm totally perfect, just as I am. It can be a difficult feat to truly embrace who we are, but it is necessary if we ever want to find true joy and contentment.

"The moment will arrive when you are comfortable with who you are, and what you are — bald or old or fat or poor, successful or struggling — when you don't feel the need to apologize for anything or to deny anything. To be comfortable in your own skin is the beginning of strength."

— Charles Handy

January 5

I am surrounded by love and support.

No matter what, I know that I have numerous people in my life who love and support me — family, friends, or even strangers. These vital relationships motivate me to never give up when things get tough and to focus on achieving success. They are the wind beneath my wings.

January 6

I am attracting abundance.

In my daily life, I might just be getting by — but when it comes to attracting and manifesting what I want in life, I know I am pursuing the right path.

"Plant seeds of happiness, hope, success, and love; it will all come back to you in abundance. This is the law of nature."

— Steve Maraboli

In short, feeling bountiful is a reflection of how I feel like abundance is flowing through my life.

January 7

I am not my mistakes.

Despite the fact that I make mistakes, it does not define who I am. It's important for me to recognize my positive attributes and take away lessons from any errors rather than ruminating on them. This reminder is here to help me stay focused on the good things about myself despite whatever missteps may occur in life.

January 8

I am thankful for my mindset.

I am thankful for my unique perspective, thought process, and ability to make life-altering decisions. Although I may face hardships and adversity at times, I continue to find beauty in the world, and those around me. It's remarkable how a constructive outlook can help conquer obstacles and sustain positivity during difficult situations.

January 9

I am grateful for my body.

I feel proud and content with my body, the way I appear, and how I live. It's okay to be thankful for all of me — every part of my physical being, each emotion that has come over me, even the tiny moments or stories that have led up to this moment right now. These little things may seem insignificant, but they have created something wonderful out of who I am today. There is no one else like me.

January 10

I am alive and vibrant.

As I wake up each morning, I am reminded of how blessed and fortunate I am to be alive. Each day is a new opportunity for success — one that should not go wasted. By making the most of my life with its countless possibilities, I can make sure that no single moment goes unused.

January 11

I am strong.

At times when it seems I can't carry on, I take a moment to recognize my inner strength — strength that at times even surpasses what I ever imagined. My past has made me resilient, and I am confident that this, too, shall pass.

January 12

I have everything I need to succeed.

I will unleash my natural talents and gifts to propel me closer to my ambitions. By utilizing them, I can accomplish any goal or dream I have set for myself. When those inevitable negative thoughts start swirling around in the back of my mind, instead of getting caught up in it all, I'll focus on how fortunate and privileged I am, which gives me a better chance at success.

January 13

I choose to focus on the positive.

Rather than dwelling on the negative, I choose to focus my attention and energy on the positive. Negativity may be unavoidable at times, but it is up to me how much of an influence it has over my life; I strive to keep a mindset that looks for all the good things in existence and stays hopeful about what lies ahead.

January 14

I am valuable just as I am.

No matter what I may have heard my entire life, no matter if the numbers and statistics portray me as "below average" or that I lack something valuable to society; none of those things even compare to how content and satisfied I am with myself and my life. That is all that really matters in the end.

January 15

I am talented.

"The person born with a talent they are meant to use will find their greatest happiness in using it."

— Johann Wolfgang von Goethe

January 16

I consider myself to be a fantastic person.

I possess ultimate control over my own thoughts, which is why I choose to think highly of myself — because if not me, then who? Negative self-dialogue will eventually manifest into a self-fulfilling prophecy. Therefore, it's essential that I strive to keep my mindset positive each and every day.

January 17

I will not let my past define me.

Rather than allowing my past to control me, I am actively learning from it. This helps free me up to live a joyous and satisfying life, not one that is limited by bad experiences. Rather than accepting the status quo of yesterday, today I choose to embrace tomorrow with enthusiasm and hope.

January 18

I am not perfect and that's okay.

Perfection can be an unattainable goal, but that doesn't mean I should shy away from my imperfections. Instead of being ashamed of them, I use them to my advantage and recognize how they make me undeniably unique.

January 19

I am a caring friend.

I treasure my friends and care deeply for them, so I don't hesitate to show them support during their tough moments. Going the extra mile to make sure they feel appreciated is something I prioritize because our shared friendship is invaluable.

January 20

I have a lot to offer the world.

I am overflowing with gifts, from my skills and time to a compassionate ear. Even more, I recognize that what I have is invaluable - greater than anything money can buy — and it's so meaningful to give this away for the betterment of all. There is never any hesitation in my heart because I know wholeheartedly, that everywhere I go, somebody will benefit from my presence.

January 21

I am resilient.

Despite whatever life throws my way, I am resilient and capable of overcoming any obstacle. My steadfastness has pushed me through difficult times before, making me an even more determined individual on the other side. As a survivor who will never surrender to defeat, I have faith that nothing can break my spirit or weaken my unwavering strength.

January 22

I am unique.

My uniqueness is something to be cherished and embraced, for there is nobody else like me in this world. I make sure to let my one-of-a-kindness burst forth so everyone can witness its sparkle. My singularity makes me valuable beyond measure, just the way I am.

January 23

I trust my inner voice.

The more I understand myself, the easier it is to trust my intuition. It can be difficult to focus on what makes me happy when other people are trying to influence me in a different direction, but if I learn how to drown out those noises and focus solely on my inner voice, then its messages will become unmistakably clear.

January 24

Not everyone has to like me and that's okay.

Although it's tempting to want to impress everyone, I cannot give in and please them all. Not every individual will be fond of me regardless of what I do or how hard I try, and that is perfectly alright. It is important for me to embrace who I am instead of conforming myself into a mold created by someone else; the fact that my uniqueness sets me apart from others should be celebrated.

January 25

My future is mine to choose.

I can create my own future, realizing my aspirations if I'm prepared to persevere and never waver. No one commands authority over my destiny but me.

January 26

I am open and honest with my feelings.

It can be nerve-wracking to expose my feelings to the world, especially if I fear being judged. Nevertheless, it is significant for me to stay true to myself by openly and honestly expressing these emotions. Doing so will allow me to establish more profound connections with others and build meaningful relationships that last over time.

January 27

I'll be precisely where I want to be in ten years.

There is no such thing as too late when it comes to pursuing my aspirations. Even if I am yet to discover what direction I want for my life, that's perfectly alright. As long as there is a plan in motion and progress is being made, the details will fall into place along the way. All that matters is that I'm on track to achieving something meaningful — whatever it may be.

January 28

I am already good enough.

Shining brightly, I am right where I need to be. Doing the utmost with what is available to me and taking pride in my accomplishments, I look ahead towards a new future and never cease striving for greatness.

January 29

I am grateful for my many blessings.

It's easy to overlook the positive in our lives, but when I pause and reflect on all that is good around me, I realize how truly fortunate I am. From my health to my family and friends — I'm grateful for so many blessings.

January 30

My light will never go out.

I am a beacon of hope in this world, and my light will never cease to burn, no matter the circumstances. I stand tall with pride for who I am and I refuse to let anyone dim my glow.

January 31

Things will get better.

"As long as you're alive, there's always a chance things will get better."

— Laini Taylor

FEBRUARY

February 1

I am filled with love and light.

"Your heart is where your inner light resides. It is part of every sacred journey to reconnect with your inner light, step into your divinity, spread the light of love before you, return to the essence of love, and inspire others to do the same."

— Molly Friedenfeld

February 2

No matter where I go, my heart is always with me.

In spite of the loneliness and unfamiliarity I may experience, I am comforted by my heart's presence. And so, no matter where in the world I go, a piece of home is always with me.

February 3

I am significant.

Despite the fact that billions of people occupy this world, there is still something unique and outstanding about each one of us. We should never feel small or insignificant because our individual contributions to society are invaluable. I know that my own personal worth possesses great value in its own right.

February 4

I radiate positive energy.

Positive thinking generates positive energy. Therefore, if I desire to emit optimistic vibes, I must start by embracing uplifting thoughts. Every day, I choose to concentrate on something that brings me joy and for which I am thankful — a simple act of reflection like this helps bring more blessings into my life.

February 5

I am brave.

Bravery isn't about being unafraid, but rather it's about having the fortitude to confront my fears. It requires tremendous courage for me to stand up for what I believe in, even when it becomes intimidating. Subsequently, I am determined not only to be brave but also never abandon myself, no matter how difficult life can seem at times.

February 6

My opinions and ideas matter.

I am unafraid to boldly express my thoughts and feelings, since they are just as valid as anyone else's. I have the right to stand up for myself and make sure that my perspective is heard. My voice matters.

February 7

I know what to hold on to and what to let go.

I often need to remind myself that I don't have control over everything, and that there are ways to learn how to let go.

Steps to learning how to let go:

1. Forgive oneself.

2. Accept what happened.

3. Let go of the hurt.

4. Focus on the future.

5. Live in the present.

February 8

I am open to new possibilities.

I am always open to new adventures and don't shy away from opportunities that take me out of my comfort zone. By taking risks, I have access to incredible experiences that may even lead me towards a newfound passion.

February 9

I am not a burden to anybody or anything.

I don't let anyone make me feel inferior or insignificant, because I know how valuable I am. Those who recognize my worth treat and love me with respect, so it's vital that I honor and cherish myself just as they do.

February 10

I will not compare myself to others.

Instead of comparing myself to others, I keep my eye on the prize and appreciate my own accomplishments. Everyone is walking their own path in life, so why not take pride in mine? By focusing on what's ahead of me, it helps me stay motivated and energized for whatever comes next.

February 11

I am patient.

Enduring through the journey is key to achieving all that I desire. Although progress might be slow, I'm determined not to lose sight of my ultimate goal and persistently work hard until I get there. Patience, indeed, is a virtue, and it will undoubtedly pay off in dividends for me someday.

February 12

I am sunshine.

Despite the weather outside, I am determined to be a ray of sunlight for someone else. My glowing optimism and good-naturedness are sure to bring some cheer into somebody's day. Today is going to be brighter because of me.

February 13

I will get good grades in school.

I am confident in my ability to excel academically with the effort I'm willing to dedicate. My smarts and hard work will ensure that I reach all of my goals.

February 14

I am the one true love of my life.

"Love yourself first, and everything else falls in line. You really have to love yourself to get anything done in this world."

— Lucille Ball

February 15

I am loved.

Regardless of what other people may think or say, I know that I am loved and cherished. To ensure my own self-confidence and security, it is essential for me to be surrounded by individuals who are supportive and loving — this makes a tremendous difference in my life.

February 16

I am kind to myself.

I am compassionate towards myself. I approach my life with love and understanding, and the difference in how I feel is remarkable.

February 17

I am thankful for what I have.

In even the most trying times, I take a moment to remember what and who I am grateful for. This helps me to understand that life isn't as dire as it might seem and appreciate everything around me more deeply. It's amazing how quickly my mood can improve when I focus on the blessings in my life instead of dwelling on the difficulties.

February 18

Every day is a chance to learn and grow.

Even as the years pass, there is no limit to how much I can grow. In order for me to stay sharp and broaden my skillset, it's essential that I am never scared of stepping out of my comfort zone in pursuit of knowledge. Today marks another chance for me to learn something new.

February 19

I will not let my fears hold me back.

Rather than succumbing to my fears, I take it upon myself to push through and confront anything that stands in my way. Although this is often intimidating, I'm proud of the courage this takes — and grateful for its rewards.

February 20

I am living in the present moment.

Cherishing the present, I don't look back on the past nor speculate about an uncertain future. Instead, I maximize every minute of my life and never forget to appreciate all that it has to offer.

February 21

I am forgiven.

Everyone has done something that they regret, yet it's how I make sense of my errors and learn from them that is significant. Instead of punishing myself for past wrongdoings, I accept the fact that everyone makes mistakes and choose to move forward with a renewed perspective. Knowing this gives me peace in knowing that no matter what happens, I am still forgiven.

February 22

My freedom to be vulnerable is precious to me.

Embracing vulnerability is a sign of strength, not frailty. It takes tremendous courage to be open and genuine about my feelings. Therefore, I treasure this aspect of myself that makes me who I am.

February 23

I am allowed to feel all of my emotions.

I don't repress my emotions — I allow them to be expressed. No matter what they may be, it's acceptable for me to feel how I do. It doesn't have to always stick with being good or bad; sometimes, it's a mixture of both, and that is okay too.

February 24

I will not be defined by other people's expectations.

I refuse to define myself based on anyone else's expectations. I'm my own person and will always strive for self-determination and autonomy in life. My story is mine, not someone else's — no one gets to dictate how it unfolds but me.

February 25

I will not be afraid to take risks.

Taking risks is a necessary part of life, so I actively embrace it. When presented with new opportunities and experiences, I dive in wholeheartedly. Although the outcome may be unknown or unpredictable at times, that just adds to the thrill.

February 26

Rest is essential for growth, for love, and for life.

Rest is a requirement, not an indulgence. Without sufficient time to rest and relax, I cannot thrive, love, or even exist. Therefore, I commit to getting enough downtime every day so that my body and mind can be restored. Doing this will undoubtedly bring me immense gratitude in the long run.

February 27

I am worthy of taking up space.

I am worthy of occupying space. No one has the authority to make me feel like I should not be here, or that my presence is undeserved. I matter and have a right to exist.

February 28

I am a work of art.

Crafting art is a journey of self-expression, and I am proud to be on the path toward growth. As I progress through life, my artwork will also continue to evolve.

February 29

I am authentic.

"As I began to love myself I found that anguish and emotional suffering are only warning signs that I was living against my own truth. Today, I know this is 'authenticity'."

— Charlie Chaplin

MARCH

March 1

There is no greater person to be than myself.

"Be yourself; everyone else is already taken."

———— Oscar Wilde

As the only one who knows what it's like to be me, I am responsible for being my best self. Promoting and supporting myself is key to realizing my full potential, so I always strive for excellence while keeping faith in my abilities.

March 2

I accept compliments with grace and gratitude.

When someone acknowledges my accomplishments and compliments me, it's an opportunity to celebrate myself. I should take in all the kind words humbly with gratefulness, recognizing that I am worthy of them.

March 3

Today I am a leader.

Today, I proudly accept the challenge of taking command and becoming a leader that others can rely on. My self-assurance in my capabilities gives me comfort in knowing that I am capable of making a positive impact. With unwavering courage, I will guide the way forward.

March 4

I have what it takes to succeed.

Instead of idly wishing for success, I strive to attain it since I am capable and determined enough to make my ambitions a reality. In fact, through my skillset, enthusiasm, and willpower — I have full faith in myself that anything is possible.

March 5

It is okay not to know everything.

I'm only human, and it's perfectly reasonable for me not to have all of the answers. There is no shame in still learning and growing, so I should be kinder to myself when I don't have immediate solutions. Instead of being hard on myself, I can always ask others for help if needed.

March 6

My opinion of myself is the only one that matters.

Oftentimes, we are tempted to take into consideration the thoughts of those around us and let their opinions shape our views of ourselves. However, I have come to realize that it is my own self-image which matters most. I choose to embrace the positivity in life by focusing on what truly makes me feel secure and confident about who I am.

March 7

I am in control of my life.

My life is my own to command. As the captain of the ship, I am responsible for setting its course and determining where it sails.

I take ownership of my destiny and chart a course that steers me toward success.

March 8

I am not afraid to speak my mind.

I have the right to express my views and convictions without fear of reproach. While I may not always agree with the opinions of others, this does not preclude me from respecting their right to differ in opinion. It is by using our voices that we can strive towards creating a better future for all.

March 9

I am special.

There is great beauty and strength in my individuality, one that I take pride in. These are qualities and skills that nobody else possesses. They make me who I am. And so, instead of hiding them away, I celebrate my uniqueness and use it to work for me.

March 10

I can make a difference.

"If you believe you can make a difference, then you will make a difference. Believe in yourself, your family and your community and you will win."

— Lindsay Fox

March 11

I can do tough things.

Life may be full of obstacles, yet I am confident that with dedication and commitment, I can overcome them. Nothing frightens me because no matter what life throws my way, I know that if I try hard enough — anything is possible. The mantra "I can do tough things" encourages me to persistently pursue any challenge thrown my way.

March 12

I choose to be happy today.

With every decision I make, it is up to me whether I choose happiness or misery. Therefore, today and from this point onward, I am taking action that will bring joy into my life. By recognizing the power of choice lies in my hands alone, enabling myself to live a contented lifestyle has become achievable for me.

March 13

I have the power to care for my own needs and sentiments.

While it's beneficial to lean on others for support, I shouldn't be dependent on them. Rather, it is essential that I understand how to look after myself and my well-being — both physically and emotionally. When needed, I should be able to provide the necessary care without somebody else doing so for me.

March 14

I will not seek validation from others.

I believe that my worth as a human being has nothing to do with the opinion of others. I value myself and accept who I am, without relying on external affirmation. Instead, I strive to build self-love within and recognize my intrinsic self-worth regardless of outside influences.

March 15

I deserve to have friends who are kind to me.

I'm not willing to accept anything less than the respect I deserve, and if my friends aren't treating me with kindness, then it's time for them to go. Making new connections is far more fulfilling when they appreciate you as you are and treat you with dignified consideration.

March 16

I will not give up on myself.

Despite difficult times, I am constantly reminded that I possess the power to persevere. My resilience, strength, and determination are invaluable assets; never allowing myself or my aspirations to surrender in defeat.

March 17

I am authentic.

"Always be a first rate version of yourself and not a second rate version of someone else."

— Judy Garland

March 18

The future is full of delightful surprises.

Although I have no way of knowing what lies ahead for me, exactly where I will find myself in the years to come, or who I may meet along the way, that does not stop me from taking every opportunity presented to me and living each day as if it were my last.

March 19

I make smart decisions.

Choosing the right path in life isn't just about knowing what is right or wrong - it's also about doing the best thing. The more morally sound decisions I make, the fewer regrets and disappointments I will have. Life isn't only a result of my actions, but also a consequence of inaction. After all, we are all defined by our choices.

March 20

Problems are exciting challenges to me.

Instead of seeing obstacles as roadblocks, I view them as opportunities. Each challenge that comes my way is an opportunity to mature and gain knowledge. Far from being intimidated by problems, I'm actually invigorated at the prospect of overcoming challenges and solving difficult issues.

March 21

I am grateful for my many blessings.

I am filled with immense gratitude for the many blessings I receive on a daily basis. From having a secure home and sound body to being surrounded by people who adore me – these are just some of the things that make my life so incredibly special. Additionally, I'm blessed with optimal health, an intelligent mind, and a gentle spirit.

March 22

I am confident in my abilities.

I embrace every challenge that life presents me with assurance. I'm armed to the teeth with my skills and resources, which give me a sense of confidence as I push toward fulfilling all of my dreams.

March 23

Even my so-called "flaws" have benefits.

Even though I'm familiar with my shortcomings, it turns out they're actually quite valuable. My so-called "flaws" are essential strengths in disguise and can be used to help me succeed. Therefore, I've learned to accept them and use them as an asset.

March 24

I am safe and sound.

Regardless of the circumstances occurring around me, I can always rely on my own inner strength and courage to protect myself. When life throws curveballs my way, I take a deep breath and relax with the assurance that everything will be alright.

March 25

Others look to me for inspiration.

As a natural leader, I have earned the confidence of those around me. My determination and strength are admired by my peers, who come to me for direction and encouragement in their lives. With that comes an understanding that I know where I'm headed -and they feel reassured knowing it's in the right direction.

March 26

I always act with integrity.

Integrity and truth are of the utmost importance to me in all interactions with others. I am ever mindful not to exploit individuals, always treating them with courtesy and respect. As a result, people recognize that they can trust me without reservation — so much so that many confide in me when facing difficult decisions or dilemmas.

March 27

I attract only positive energy.

I am an emblem of positivity and only allow those who radiate love, support, and kindness into my life. I shield myself from anything negative, drawing in only good energy that will help me grow. All things positive are naturally drawn to me like a magnet.

March 28

I always stay true to myself.

I never alter my beliefs or the core of who I am for anyone, no matter what. I stand firmly in pride and self-assurance when it comes to my distinctive identity. It is essential that I remember that being myself is more than enough; there's no need to mimic someone else's version of perfection.

March 29

I am comfortable in any situation.

I have unshakable self-esteem and never hesitate to express my opinions or defend myself. Regardless of the context, I am at ease with every situation that comes my way, understanding that I can accomplish anything life throws at me.

March 30

I am helpful.

The first step is to be helpful in whatever way I can.

Kindness is essential to being a great person. We often become so entrenched in our own lives that we forget there are others around us who could use help as well. It's significant to remember that the success of one relies on the help and support of many.

March 31

I am a dreamer.

"Without leaps of imagination or dreaming, we lose the excitement of possibilities. Dreaming, after all, is a form of planning."

—— Gloria Steinem

APRIL

April 1

I am making a difference today.

I don't have to transform the world in order to make an impact. I'm making a difference, no matter how small. Each day, I do something good for another person — even if it's just saying something nice or offering a listening ear. By doing this, I know that my efforts are paying off and helping others in some way.

April 2

Good things are coming my way.

I'm open to experiencing all the positivity and abundance that life has in store for me. I trust that the universe will provide me with what I need, and so I graciously welcome any opportunities or blessings on my journey toward realizing my biggest dreams.

April 3

I am ready to learn new things.

"Always walk through life as if you have something new to learn and you will."

— Vernon Howard

April 4

I believe in myself.

With unwavering faith in my capabilities, I am more than confident that I can bring my dreams to life. My steadfast trust in myself gives me the power to create an extraordinary life for myself and those around me.

April 5

I am grateful for all the good in my life.

There is an abundance of things to be thankful for in my life that I cannot possibly enumerate them all. From having good health and amazing family members and friends, to the opportunity to pursue my goals and make a positive difference, I am filled with appreciation for all these blessings bestowed upon me.

April 6

I am courageous.

I am not afraid to seize an opportunity when it comes knocking.

I am not afraid to stand up for what I believe in.

I am not afraid to follow my heart.

I am courageous and I live life to the fullest.

April 7

I celebrate my creativity.

I am creative! As a teen, it is essential for me to explore and showcase my creativity. It doesn't matter if I'm painting, writing, or even dancing; the key point here is that I make time for myself in order to foster my creative spirit. This kind of self-expression allows me to find joy and comfort within myself because it's an integral part of who I am as a person.

April 8

I am making progress every day.

I am making tireless efforts to better myself and my life. With each passing day, I come closer to fulfilling all of my desires. My commitment to self-improvement is unwavering, and I trust that whatever objectives I set for myself will be accomplished in due time.

April 9

I trust myself.

Knowing myself better than anyone else, I am aware of my strengths and weaknesses. Understanding what I'm capable of, I trust in myself to make the right decisions by listening to my heart and following my intuition. With this confidence that only comes from self-awareness, I can rest assured that whatever choices come out of it will be for the best.

April 10

I am staying positive no matter what.

Instead of letting the difficulties and adversities discourage me, I keep my chin up and persist. Every dark cloud has a glimmer of hope; hence, I stay optimistic and will eventually come out triumphant in the end.

April 11

Negative emotions will pass.

Even when I am not feeling my best, it's important to remember that all feelings are fleeting. Before long, the bad ones will come and go too. That said, I choose to focus on the positive in life for which I'm grateful. This keeps me grounded even on those tougher days.

April 12

I am someone who is fun to be around.

I live by the mantra that life is too precious to be anything but joyous. Therefore, I strive to make myself and others around me as contented as possible — I am a ball of energy who takes pleasure in making people smile.

April 13

I have everything I need within me.

I am my best ally and confidant. Every resource I will ever need is already inside me, ready to help me reach the heights of success that I dream of. With confidence in myself, I know that any barrier can be conquered. Knowing this gives me strength, a power like no other, to accomplish all the goals I set for myself.

April 14

I am lucky to have supportive friends.

I feel so fortunate and thankful to have the incredible friends that I do. They're always there for me no matter what, offering their love and support in good times as well as bad — they are truly priceless.

April 15

Today is a gift, and I am going to make the most of it.

I am only given one life, and I vow to make the most of it. Each day brings something new, so why not appreciate that gift? My existence serves a purpose in this world, and I aim to live my life with passion, vigor, and joy! Every second is precious — seize it!

April 16

The more I practice, the better I become.

I understand that progressing toward greatness in anything I do will take time, dedication, and practice. That's why I never get discouraged. Instead, I keep perfecting my skills until I reach the level of success I desire. Even the most successful people had to start somewhere — including me.

April 17

I am always growing and improving.

At any age, I can continue to learn and improve. Growing every day, my skills and knowledge are constantly widening, allowing me to become the best version of myself possible.

April 18

I take responsibility for my own happiness.

I'm grateful for the opportunities I've been given and where I am in life. Achieving greater contentment is totally up to me, from taking accountability for my joy and designing a lifestyle that brings true gratification.

April 19

I am willing to take chances.

> "Life is about taking chances, trying new things, having fun, making mistakes and learning from it."
>
> — Anonymous

April 20

My loved ones can always count on me.

Those important to me know that whether they need help, advice, or a shoulder to lean on, I'm always there for them. My reliability and unyielding support have earned the appreciation of my loved ones, who can trust I'll be by their side no matter what.

April 21

I am loyal.

I am devoted to the things I cherish and would never compromise my beliefs. My loyalty to my family, friends, and values is unwavering. They can always trust that I'll be there for them in their time of need.

April 22

I am committed to living my best life.

I am eager to live the best life possible and nothing less. I'm dedicated to personal growth, putting in all the effort needed to attain my goals. No matter how much dedication it calls for, I will not settle until I have achieved what is set before me.

April 23

I am a hard-worker.

In order to reach my aspirations, I realize that hard work and dedication are required. Laziness will not help me get anywhere in life; only through sheer determination and devotion can I hope for success. As a steadfast individual with unwavering ambition, nothing can stand in the way of reaching my goals.

April 24

Beauty comes in a variety of shapes and sizes.

I no longer concern myself with my frame or size. Beauty isn't limited to physical appearance; it's the result of a culmination of confidence, contentment, and self-care. So I'm disregarding my insecurities and welcoming the beauty within me.

April 25

I fill my day with hope.

In a world that can often feel bleak, hope is more important now than ever before. It's the beacon of light to help me recognize the goodness and beauty amidst the darkness. If I'm struggling to identify joy, then hope will provide guidance in finding it again.

April 26

I'm not trying to fit in since I was created to stand out.

I possess a special skill, something that is solely and completely mine. I may not be the quickest or most intelligent person out there, but it's alright because I have my own individual traits and viewpoint; although different from others, this distinctiveness makes me mean to shine in this world.

April 27

All my problems have solutions.

In our ever-challenging world, it's critical to remind ourselves that there are always solutions. These times can be emotionally trying, and knowing we're not alone is invaluable. So let us start by recognizing that other people face the same problems as ours, and no matter how complex they may seem, resilient hope prevails.

April 28

My ideas are valued.

I have the power to make a difference and inspire others, for my ideas are valuable. I am endlessly grateful for being acknowledged and granted the possibility of articulating my thoughts that not merely get accepted but also put into practice. With this in mind, I can confidently assert that I possess what it takes to revolutionize our world.

April 29

I am honest.

I am not afraid to tell the truth, no matter what.

"Honesty is the fastest way to prevent a mistake from turning into a failure."

— James Altucher

April 30

I have the power to make my dreams come true.

I have my own special aspirations, and even though it can be difficult to reach them at times, I refuse to give up. My first step is always believing in myself and knowing that I am capable of making these ambitions a reality. After that comes the actual work

— taking those crucial steps toward realizing what I desire most will surely bring me closer to success!

MAY

May 1

I will pursue my aspirations with enthusiasm and joy.

I am confident in my capabilities and trust that I can achieve extraordinary feats. Even if the objectives ahead of me seem far-fetched, I refuse to give up on them. By staying hopeful and dedicating myself to working hard, nothing is beyond my reach. With enthusiasm and vigor, I will strive for what lies before me with unwavering dedication.

May 2

I get better everyday.

Determined to become the best version of myself, I am devoted to continuously learning and developing. With each passing day, my wisdom expands along with my strength. As a result, I'm gradually transforming into who I desire to be.

May 3

I cherish my body because it is strong and healthy.

My body is an awe-inspiring instrument, enabling me to do remarkable things. I'm fortunate for my good health and physicality — treasuring it and providing the best care possible.

May 4

I am proud of myself.

I am immensely proud of my accomplishments, as I have worked tirelessly to achieve them.

May 5

I will share my successes with others.

Whenever I achieve something, I'm not afraid to share it with others. After all, my success is something that I can be proud of.

May 6

I am intelligent.

I am an intelligent, hard-working individual, and I recognize that anything is achievable with dedication and determination. My capabilities are limitless. No matter what dream lies ahead of me, as long as I put in the effort, nothing can stand in my way.

May 7

I will not let anyone bring me down.

Nobody can take away my self-worth or dictate the contentment in my life. I possess ultimate control over how happy I choose to be and I will refuse to let anyone else affect that by judging me.

May 8

I can say 'no' if I don't want to do something.

I will not be forced into doing something just because someone else wants me to. I have the right to say "no" if I don't want to do something. Prioritizing my joy is more essential than pleasing anyone else.

May 9

My pals are not always right.

I'm going to take the time to think for myself and not just agree with whatever my friends say. Just because they find something appealing doesn't mean that I have to as well; instead, I will make decisions based on what works best for me.

May 10

I am grateful for my natural talents.

From the day I was born, my unique abilities and talents have been a blessing. I am proud of them and will put forth my best effort to utilize them with excellence. Instead of worrying about how others may measure up, I remain confident in myself; no one has the right to make me feel inferior.

May 11

I enjoy being helpful.

I take pleasure in assisting others and I always attempt to offer a helping hand where I can. Whether it's carrying groceries for an elderly neighbor or tutoring a classmate, being of service is rewarding work.

May 12

I will not give up easily.

In moments of difficulty, I will never surrender. My strength and perseverance are unwavering; nothing can stop me from accomplishing my ambitions. No challenge is too insurmountable for me to overcome with resilience — I am steadfast and determined.

May 13

I'm going to enjoy my youth.

"Youth comes but once in a lifetime."

— Henry Wadsworth Longfellow

May 14

I'm not in a hurry; I've got plenty of time.

Rather than frantically sprinting through life, I'm going to take a deep breath and savor the experience. There is no need to rush; all that matters is that I enjoy every stage of my journey.

May 15

I am sufficient.

I am content in my life. I don't need anyone else's approval to feel good about myself. My own self-approval is the only thing that gives me a sense of satisfaction and joy. It is all that matters.

May 16

I don't need drugs or alcohol to have a good time.

I can have just as much fun without substances. I don't need a crutch to enjoy myself. I'm confident and capable of finding pleasure in life without the use of drugs or alcohol.

May 17

I will not let my fears hold me back.

Instead of allowing my apprehensions to take the wheel, I will be courageous and tackle them head-on. By doing this, I am sure that I can conquer any fear standing in my way.

May 18

I will be assertive when I need to be.

No longer will I allow myself to be taken advantage of. Instead, I will take a stand and articulate my needs. Whenever it is necessary, I am now bold enough to express what's in my heart without hesitation or fear.

May 19

I am proud to represent the ideals that are valuable to me.

I have faith in my convictions and am not afraid to speak up for what I believe. My words are always heard, respected, and taken into consideration by those around me. By taking action on my passions, I give others the courage to go after their own aspirations without fear of failure or judgment.

May 20

I am grateful for the progress I have made.

I have come a long way, and although there is still much to be done, I am proud of the progress I have made. Every day, my ambitions are being realized while at the same time transforming me into who I want to become.

May 21

I am in control of my thoughts and emotions.

The choices I make define my state of mind, and I am solely in control over my own joy. No one has the capability to dictate how things will go for me; it's completely up to me to fashion the life that I desire.

May 22

I'm in charge of my technology.

I am in control of how much time I spend on my devices, and I never let myself become enslaved by them. When it comes to technology, I strive for a balanced relationship—using my phone, tablet, or computer responsibly and putting them aside when finished.

May 23

I don't give up when obstacles appear.

With a tenacious attitude and unrelenting spirit, I never shy away from difficult problems. Instead, I embrace any challenge with vigor and determination as an opportunity to rise above. Obstacles are seen only as chances to prove my strength — not hindrances that put me at bay.

May 24

I take breaks when I need to.

I understand the importance of taking a break every now and then. I give myself permission to rest and rejuvenate when I need to. Taking the time to nurture my own needs, I pay attention to my body's cues. My physical and emotional health depends on regularly pausing for much-needed breaks.

May 25

I seek new skills.

My zest for learning never ends; I'm ever-evolving as a person. Growing my capabilities and mastering new skills is an ongoing endeavor of mine. Each day, I am becoming a greater version of myself than the day before.

May 26

I always put my best foot forward in everything I do.

I am passionate and dedicated in everything I do, no matter how small or large the task is. My commitment to success drives me to work diligently towards achieving excellence.

May 27

I don't sweat the small stuff.

I am aware that most things in life are not worth stressing over. Instead, I choose to channel my energy towards the aspects of life that actually count. Therefore, I prefer to let go of all the small insignificant details and instead focus on what truly matters.

May 28

Every time I fall, I get up.

"Our greatest glory is not in never failing, but in rising every time we fail."

— Confucius

May 29

I trust my instincts.

I trust my intuition, as I know it has never let me down. My inner guidance system is strong and powerful. Therefore, I listen to my gut and follow my heart without fail — for it rarely steers me wrong.

May 30

I am comfortable with change.

I recognize that change is constantly occurring and I'm willing to roll with the punches. My degree of flexibility allows me to adjust quickly while embracing life's various changes.

May 31

I take time for myself.

Every day, I commit to offering myself quality time. Doing enjoyable activities that make me feel radiant is integral to keeping my health in peak condition. By scheduling exclusive 'me' moments regularly, both my body and soul stay nourished.

JUNE

June 1

Today is going to be a fantastic day.

To kick the day off on a high note, I'll make sure to give my best friend a hefty pat on the back and take an unforgettable selfie at their door. Then it's time for some sumptuous coffee with one of our personally beloved croissants before we get comfortable and relish in an amazing book together. Then, maybe even discuss the plot twists in a movie we both enjoyed watching recently.

June 2

I can do challenging tasks.

My philosophy is that no dream should be viewed as too unattainable. The bigger the challenge, the more vigorous my desire to accomplish it becomes. Fueled by an ambitious attitude and a fierce competitive edge, I strive for new heights while also learning valuable capabilities along the way. My curious spirit combined with creativity empowers me to take even my wildest aspirations and turn them into reality.

June 3

I show empathy.

I am an individual who is profoundly understanding of those around me, even the strangers I have yet to meet. Every time someone does something or asks a question that perplexes me, I try my hardest to understand their point-of-view and show them kindness in return. That's how I express empathy for others.

June 4

My sentiments are valid.

I will no longer allow the opinion of others to supersede what I know is right for me and my life. Furthermore, it's inconsiderate for someone else to take liberties in deciding another person's fate without getting a real sense of who they are first.

June 5

I let go of my anxieties.

Shedding my anxieties was not a difficult task for me. Rather, forming the habit of embracing simplicity made all the difference. The most efficient approach to reducing stress is tackling it head-on and taking preventive measures instead of fretting over them.

June 6

My day will begin with joy and thankfulness.

I am profoundly thankful for my health and all the remarkable things I have been able to do with my body. Moreover, I extend deep appreciation to those who have offered me assistance so far on this journey of mine — as well as an eagerness to help others when possible.

June 7

I accept and cherish people as they are.

I'm not swayed by outward appearances, clothes, or demeanor; I give my love unconditionally and without any pre-set limits. It doesn't matter if someone deserves it — all that matters to me is what's in my heart for them.

June 8

My only opponent is myself.

As a highly competitive individual, I recognize the importance of exercising mindfulness when my zeal for success becomes too strong. Every time I reprimand myself for not achieving something, it is an uplifting reminder of my identity and why it's so important to keep pursuing my ambitions.

June 9

I refrain from criticizing myself

It's easy to become too hard on ourselves. However, I'm discovering that this isn't necessarily a helpful approach. Instead of fixating on my imperfections and shortfalls, I'm now emphasizing the attributes which make me special: My qualities. By acknowledging these assets, I can construct them into an effective platform for accomplishing success — both with myself as well as in relation to others.

June 10

I'm proud of my outspoken persona.

I'm grateful for the right to express my ideas openly, which is something everyone should learn about and value. This freedom of speech has enabled me to speak up for what I believe in, and for that, I am immensely proud.

June 11

I have boundless potential for growth.

The world has so much to offer me that I can't wait to explore it and expand my knowledge. It is an enriching experience for me, as a changemaker who loves learning about new things, growing in life, and making progress on personal goals. After each adventure or milestone reached along the way, I find myself more fulfilled than ever before.

June 12

I make wise decisions in my life.

Life can be daunting and present us with decisions that will determine how our future unfolds. However, I believe we all have the power to choose wisely and make choices in life that will steer away from regret. When I'm mindful of my actions and opt for wisdom, it's almost guaranteed to lead me down a path where fulfillment is achieved instead of mediocrity taking its place.

June 13

I am on the right path.

"If you're walking down the right path and you're willing to keep walking, eventually you'll make progress."

— Barack Obama

June 14

I have the freedom to be loud without hurting others.

I freely express myself in ways that come naturally to me, whether it's through writing, art, music, fashion, or speaking my truth. I know everyone doesn't always agree with me, and that's okay. We're all on our own journey trying to make sense of things from our perspective. The most important thing is living life authentically with integrity and respecting others the way I want to be respected.

June 15

I will not make excuses.

Instead of making excuses for my mistakes and missed chances, I will learn from them. By understanding what went awry and how to avoid it in the future, I am taking a proactive approach to personal growth.

June 16

I am not selfish.

I'm not driven by ego, ambition, or greed because I comprehend that being selfish is to simply act with disregard for those around me. To be selfish is to stifle growth and stunt development. What really brings joy and prosperity are qualities such as kindness, generosity, and friendliness — which often yield far greater results than any individual who only values themselves above all else.

June 17

I love my smile.

I love my smile. It's a big part of who I am. I know it plays a big role in how people judge me, but that's OK. I'm an optimist and believe we shouldn't let others dictate how we should feel about ourselves.

So, I'll keep smiling and hope that more people will smile back.

June 18

My mistakes help me learn and grow.

Perfection is not a goal of mine, as I'm more interested in learning and growing from my mistakes. Rather than remaining stuck on any pitfalls I experience, it's far better to take them into account and then move forward with the valuable lessons they've taught me — for which there are likely countless opportunities ahead.

June 19

I'm going to take a chance.

I'm pushing myself out of my comfort zone to achieve something I've always yearned for, and even if it doesn't turn out as planned, attempting is still a success. It's now or never; let the journey begin.

June 20

I'm going to make the best decisions for me.

Trusting my inherent wisdom, I shall always listen to myself and make decisions that are in line with what makes ME happy. My intuition is strong and guiding me toward the right path - this is MY life, so I will not be swayed by anyone else's beliefs or opinions. By staying true to myself, I know that whatever choices I make are for the best.

June 21

My possibilities are limitless.

I refuse to let anything stand in my way of meeting any goal I set for myself. The only obstacle keeping me from success is my own mindset, so I will strive even harder than ever before and find out how far I can go. There's nothing hindering me from hitting new heights.

June 22

I can take deep breaths to calm myself down.

When I find myself overwhelmed with stress, I turn to deep breathing as an instant remedy. It's a straightforward way for me to feel more centered and relaxed. After inhaling deeply several times, my mindset clears so that I am able to make wise decisions in the heat of the moment.

June 23

I will not allow my emotions to control me.

Rather than allowing my emotions to dictate how I feel and react, I take control of them. No longer will I be a victim of my own feelings; instead, by mastering them, they can serve me as an advantage in life.

June 24

I have inner strengths that I can rely on.

On those days when I'm feeling down, it's crucial to remind myself that my excuses don't define me. I can always access the internal strength and resilience within, which will equip me with everything necessary to traverse any adversity life throws at me.

June 25

I can do better next time.

I'm aware that I don't have to be perfect for me to reach my desired outcome. If I make a mistake, it's an opportunity for learning and growth. So instead of giving up or caving into failure, I will take the lesson in stride and keep pushing toward success while doing my absolute best.

June 26

I am a genuine person.

I have no fear in exhibiting who I am — genuine, honest, and unequivocally real. Instead of masking myself with fakery, I'm my own person and wear it proudly. People find me alluring for being true to myself and they recognize that authenticity goes a long way.

June 27

I refuse to give up on myself.

Giving up is never an option for me because I have the courage to keep going despite failure being part of success' path. My faith in myself gives me strength regardless of how often I fall during this journey; therefore, persistence will be key as long as there's breath within my lungs.

June 28

I can show appreciation to people who matter to me.

I'm deeply grateful for the people in my life who mean so much to me. Showing them how thankful I am is important to me, which is why I make sure to be kind, considerate, and supportive of them at all times. They know that their presence has a positive impact on my life, and I never miss an opportunity to let them know just how special they are.

June 29

Anything is possible.

"With hard work and dedication, anything is possible."

— Timothy Weah

June 30

Today I am going to shine brightly.

I am determined to shine brightly today. With a smile on my face and optimism in my heart, I will spread joy and positivity that is sure to attract wonderful people into my life. Today is truly set up for greatness.

JULY

July 1

The world is my oyster.

I'm embarking on a journey to explore the breadth of the world and all its wonders. I'm eager to immerse myself in new cultures, meet fascinating people, and become enlightened by experiences far beyond what I know now. With so much beauty awaiting my discovery, it's time for me to finally begin this adventure.

July 2

I deserve only the best.

By persistently nurturing a positive and uplifting mindset, I am guaranteed to receive everything that I deserve and more. In doing so, my life will be full of joyous contentment.

July 3

There is no such thing as an impossible dream.

No matter the difficulty of my dreams, I will never abandon them. If I firmly believe in something and put forth ample effort, anything is attainable. Thus, I remain determined to achieve greatness despite how difficult it may be at times.

July 4

I am free to be whoever I want to be.

I will never let anyone else dictate who I am or how I should live my life. This is my journey, and it's up to me alone to shape and express myself as I desire. No one has the power to make decisions for me — these choices are mine, and only mine.

July 5

Everything will be okay.

"If something does go wrong, here is my advice, keep calm and carry on, and eventually everything will fall back in place."

— Maira Kalman

July 6

With every breath, I feel more at ease.

Inhale, exhale. Inhale, exhale.

I inhale deeply and exhale slowly, feeling the stress evaporate from my body. With each breath I take, I find myself becoming more relaxed and composed. As I focus on my breathing pattern, all other anxieties drift out of consciousness.

July 7

I will work through my struggles.

Though life may have its fair share of obstacles, I am certain that I possess the resilience and strength to conquer them. With courage and determination, no challenge is too great for me as I will take it on with conviction and emerge a more powerful version of myself.

July 8

I will carve a name for myself.

I am determined to be different and unique. I will strive to make a lasting impression, build an enviable reputation, and generate success by exercising my creative passion.

July 9

I am passionate about my craft.

I'm devoted to reaching my highest potential. I always invest an immense amount of effort into all that I do, and constantly work on bettering myself and expanding my knowledge. My ardor spurs me on to achieve the best that I can be.

July 10

My success is inevitable.

I am unyielding in my pursuit of success. My ambition and dedication will be unwavering no matter the obstacles I may face along the way, for that is how I have been preordained to find triumph.

July 11

There is nothing wrong with not knowing everything.

I'm not ashamed to admit that I don't know everything, and neither should you be. It's simply impossible — even for the most knowledgeable people in the world. However, this is an opportunity to gain further knowledge instead of a limitation. I embrace learning new things and growing as much as possible.

July 12

I am grateful for my family and friends.

I am incredibly blessed to be surrounded by a wonderful and caring family and friends. In all of life's endeavors, they are there for me without fail — I could not have asked for better people in my life. I treasure their presence with me every day.

July 13

I will not take things for granted.

I'm deeply thankful for all of the moments, experiences, and people who enter my life. I will actively embrace every positive experience and learn from any negative one that comes my way. Not a single person or thing will be taken lightly as I acknowledge how fortunate I am in this world.

July 14

I will find beauty in the world around me.

Every day, I will open my eyes to the awe-inspiring beauty that surrounds me. The world is a place full of amazement and grandeur; never growing tired of discovering it. No matter where I go, there is beauty — and I am determined to find it.

July 15

I am ready to take on hardships.

Armed with my inner strength and confidence, I am empowered to take on any hardships that life throws at me. There is nothing too daunting for me to overcome. Bring it on!

July 16

I write my own destiny.

"Destiny is no matter of chance. It is a matter of choice. It is not a thing to be waited for, it is a thing to be achieved."

— William Jennings Bryan

July 17

I have faith in my abilities.

Believing in myself and envisioning my potential is the foundation to everything I do. Self-confidence, at its core, requires me to firmly trust what I can accomplish. It gives me the assurance that all my goals are attainable and makes me proud of who I am. It motivates me to reach for heights undreamt of instead of settling for mediocrity or a simple status quo life — with confidence comes power.

July 18

Wonderful things are around me.

Life is abundant with stunning sunsets, fragrant cups of coffee, and kind smiles from strangers — all occurring around me. I recognize the beauty in these moments and savor them because this is what makes life remarkable.

July 19

I'm building my future.

I wholeheartedly believe that life should be savored and enjoyed to its fullest. I think it's important to stay motivated, take action and let those around you know what your intentions are. Writing down a vision for the future keeps me focused on creating my desired reality while reminding me of how far I've come — an effective way of keeping track of all my goals, dreams, and aspirations.

July 20

Everyday is a new beginning.

Today is a chance to make positive strides in my life and become even better than I was yesterday. Tomorrow will be an opportunity to grow further, so that I can exceed the progress made today. Each day presents me with limitless potential for advancement and improvement.

July 21

I cherish what I have been blessed with.

I am truly blessed to have an abundance of love and support from my family and friends, as well as a wealth of skills, talents, and good health. I recognize how lucky I am to possess these gifts in life, which is why it fills me with immense gratitude.

July 22

I am persevering.

I'm the type of person who doesn't back away from a challenge. No matter how difficult something may seem, I never give up and continue to pursue my goals with tenacity until they are accomplished. When confronted by obstacles, I find ways to overcome them — nothing can stop me from chasing after what it is that I want out of life.

July 23

My happiness comes from within.

I constantly remind myself that I am solely in charge of my own joy. Realizing this power is critical to embracing positivity and savoring life's moments whenever possible.

July 24

I choose love.

Sometimes life can be tough; however, I'm certain that love is the ultimate solution—whether it's shown to our family and friends or even towards strangers. Love has no boundaries. It welcomes all with open arms, no matter what kind of relationship we have with someone else.

July 25

I am loyal to the passion within me.

I ardently strive to live a life that aligns with my beliefs and values, never wavering from what I'm passionate about. With authenticity and righteousness at the core of every endeavor I undertake, there is no dream too far-fetched for me to go after.

July 26

I shall follow my dreams.

"I believe that the only courage anybody ever needs is the courage to follow your own dreams."

— Oprah Winfrey

I'm confident that pursuing my dreams is the greatest goal I can strive for, so irrespective of what anyone else believes, I'll never surrender and remain determined to reach my aspirations.

July 27

I am grateful for this day.

I'm so grateful to experience the gift of life — I never take it for granted. Not only do I have sustenance, shelter, and a community that loves me, but every single day brings with it an abundance of beauty, love, and new possibilities.

July 28

I am at peace with myself.

I wholeheartedly embrace my true self, unapologetically loving and accepting every part of me. I stand in my power with unwavering confidence and assurance.

July 29

I can reach for the stars.

I am driven to reach my aspirations, and I understand that nothing can prevent me from attaining them. I am willing to work hard and never give up on my goals. I am capable of greatness.

July 30

My thoughts create my reality.

From the very start of my day, I decide what kind of morning it will be by the thoughts that fill my mind. If I want to have a satisfactory day, then positivity is key, and alluring happy ideas should come first. However, if I wish for an extraordinary experience throughout the hours ahead, even more uplifting musings are essential. It's truly up to me — so today, I choose happiness.

July 31

I choose kindness.

No matter how others treat me, I make the conscious decision to be kind. With my actions, I strive to spread love and compassion throughout this world in order to make it a better place for us all. Kindness is an act of courage that can have profound impacts on our lives — so why not choose kindness?

AUGUST

August 1

I am committed to improving myself every day.

I'm committed to self-improvement, aiming to become the very best version of myself. I won't accept mediocrity--I desire excellence in all my endeavors and refuse to settle for anything less.

August 2

I find satisfaction in serving others.

Helping others makes me feel really good. I adore influencing other people's life. Knowing that I am making the world a better place makes me happy.

August 3

I have great qualities.

I am a caring, thoughtful, and kindhearted person. I am a nice buddy and a good listener. I'm constantly looking for ways to get better, and I'm always prepared to lend a hand.

August 4

I feed my mind with useful knowledge.

I make certain I am well-versed. Knowing something is preferable to not knowing it since it makes it difficult to determine what to do next. Knowing things is merely being knowledgeable, and being knowledgeable doesn't only mean reading. It's being able to ask the correct questions, figure out difficulties, and select the best course of action in a given circumstance.

August 5

I learn and grow from my mistakes.

Everyone slips up sometimes; however, these mistakes don't define who I am as an individual. Rather, the outcomes of my mistakes teach me valuable lessons that help to cultivate personal growth and development.

August 6

I deserve to have fun.

I'm determined to go the extra mile in all that I do, and I fully deserve a little recreation too. With this thought in mind, I refuse to feel guilty about having fun. Rather, I'm going to make sure that my life is balanced with leisure activities as well as home chores and school work.

August 7

This is the right place for me.

I'm exactly at the point where I was meant to be. Even though I haven't accomplished my aspirations yet, I am still working toward them and making steady progress. Each day brings new wisdom and opportunities for growth that propel me nearer to achieving what it is that I want in life.

August 8

My life is incredible so far, and I am not stopping.

The amazing experiences I've had thus far in life have only strengthened my ambitions to explore further. There's no end in sight for me, as I'm determined to keep pushing the boundaries and trying out new things. Life is an incredible journey, so why not make it even more memorable?

August 9

I always look at the bright side of life.

I am an optimist, believing that no matter the circumstances — good will prevail and positive outcomes are possible.

August 10

I set the bar high and work hard to reach my goals.

I refuse to settle for mediocrity and instead consistently push myself to become the best version of me possible. I'm never content with simply meeting the required standards. I strive for excellence, setting higher goals that challenge my abilities and working diligently until those targets are met.

August 11

I strive to be better every day.

"I'm better than I used to be. Better than I was yesterday. But hopefully not as good as I'll be tomorrow,"

— Marianne Williamson

August 12

I am going to make everyone proud.

I am confident that I will accomplish remarkable feats in my lifetime, and all of those who are close to me will be incredibly proud. I am going to make a difference in the world.

August 13

I always stay true to myself.

I remain steadfast in my principles and true to myself, regardless of the circumstances. I won't yield to anyone or anything that might alter who I am as a person.

August 14

I am sound and healthy.

I prioritize my physical, mental, and emotional health, continuously striving to better myself. I am proud of the soundness and energy that this commitment has brought me — it is a source of strength for which I am deeply grateful.

August 15

I have great life visions.

With bold aspirations, I am determined to make my dreams a reality. Unafraid of the unknown, I persevere in pursuit of what I truly desire out of life.

August 16

I possess excellent qualities.

I strive to be the best version of myself. I am committed to helping others, lending an ear, and offering advice. My abilities make me proud, for they are remarkable qualities that allow me to excel in friendship and compassion.

August 17

I take pride in my appearance.

I take great care in my personal grooming, recognizing how it affects those initial impressions. When I meet someone for the first time, I want to ensure that my appearance is projecting a favorable image and creating an amazing initial perception.

August 18

I am adventurous.

Whenever I get a chance, I love to set out on new ventures and explore the unknown. For me, adventure is an essential part of life. It's thrilling and exciting.

August 19

This is a glorious day.

Every day is a blessing, and I'm determined to revel in it. Today will be spectacular!

August 20

I will seize every opportunity that comes my way.

I'm ready to take hold of every opportunity that comes my way, and I shall make certain I make the most out of it.

August 21

I don't need excuses.

Instead of making excuses for my inaction, I will take full responsibility for the choices that I have made. After all, these decisions are mine alone to bear.

August 22

I am constantly expanding my knowledge and skill set.

I am passionate about pushing myself to learn more, constantly expanding my skillset, and growing with each experience. I find immense joy in continuously developing my knowledge and abilities.

August 23

My life is full of colors.

I like to take advantage of any opportunity I have to live life to the fullest. I wouldn't want my life to be any other way — it's vibrant, exciting, and full of adventure.

August 24

I will never settle for mediocrity.

I'm all-or-nothing, and will never settle for the bare minimum. I strive to be the best, no matter what it takes. Anything less than complete dedication is unacceptable. If I can't give my absolute best, then I won't do it at all.

August 25

I respect myself and others.

Everyone, without exception, deserves to be treated with kindness, consideration, and empathy. As such, I strive to demonstrate this same respect in all my interactions — both with myself and others.

August 26

I recognize my strengths and weaknesses.

As I strive to improve upon my weaknesses, it's just as important for me to recognize and express gratitude for my strengths. I understand that I possess a wealth of valuable skills and competencies which enable me to contribute greatly in various areas of life.

August 27

By taking care of myself, I can take better care of others.

If I am to be the best version of myself for others, then self-care needs to come first. From taking care of my physical and mental well-being to ensuring that I'm emotionally healthy, it's important that sometimes my own needs get prioritized so that I can properly take care of those around me. Only when we are fully nourished can we extend a helping hand in the way they need us most.

August 28

I am a good role model.

I continuously strive to be my best self so that I can serve as a beacon of motivation for those around me. By demonstrating excellence, I hope to inspire and encourage others in their own journeys.

August 29

Everything is possible.

If I put my mind to it and work hard enough, I believe everything is achievable. No matter how big or small they may be, I constantly work to attain my goals.

August 30

I am proud of my accomplishments.

I am not content to remain stationary — I have put in considerable effort to get where I am today, and will keep striving for more. Nevertheless, I cannot deny that my accomplishments are something I can take pride in.

August 31

I write my own story.

No one gets to tell me what happens in my life — I am the only one who can write my story.

SEPTEMBER

September 1

I give myself space to grow and develop.

I am always learning and growing; I never become comfortable. I brazenly carve out time in my schedule for things that I find interesting or that will help me learn new skills. Several times, my curiosity has taken me outside of my comfort zone, but that's when the magic happens.

September 2

I can provide help to someone today.

Everyone has the capacity to help others, regardless of how insignificant they may feel. It may be as simple as holding a door open or extending a sympathetic ear. I know we can all influence someone's life in a positive way.

September 3

I refuse to be ruled by my fears.

My life won't be controlled by my fears. I'm not going to let them restrict my freedom or slow me down. I'm going to confront and get through my worries.

September 4

I am a gift to others.

I'm a gift not just to myself, but to others as well. I can use my various skills and abilities to make the world a better place.

September 5

I will not be deterred by setbacks.

Even if setbacks are inevitable, I will still be able to accomplish my aspirations. I'll use the lessons I've learned from them to propel myself forward.

September 6

My mind is full of wonderful ideas.

I'm constantly brainstorming creative new ideas, and I have the courage to share my perspective with others. Moreover, I always welcome innovative suggestions.

September 7

I am dynamic.

I'm always open-minded and eager to expand my knowledge. I don't remain set in my ways, preferring instead to explore any new opportunities that come my way. As a result of being flexible and adaptive, I can switch between different situations without too much trouble at all.

September 8

It is okay to be different.

It is not only acceptable to be one of a kind, but it should also be celebrated. Instead of succumbing to the pressure to fit in with others' expectations, we all have an obligation to embrace our own individuality. Being ourselves and embracing what makes us special are invaluable gifts that should never go unrecognized or unappreciated.

September 9

I can use my talent for the benefit of the community.

I have a wide range of talents and skills, and I want to utilize these to make the world a better place. I'm going to make the most of my talents and influence the world.

September 10

I am grateful for my great parents.

I am blessed to have a remarkable and supportive set of parents who've always been there for me. My family's loyal devotion is something I will forever be thankful for — they are my unwavering pillars of strength, which makes me feel so lucky every day that they are in my life. Knowing I can rely on them anytime brings great solace to my heart.

September 11

I have a big heart.

I sincerely want to improve people's lives and change the world for the better. Even though they may not see it in themselves, I always see the best in others.

September 12

I am a great friend.

"Many people will walk in and out of your life, but only true friends will leave footprints in your heart."

— Eleanor Roosevelt

September 13

I have a keen sense of intuition.

I have a clear understanding of myself and my desired goals. My identity, who I am, and what I do, always reflect my innermost convictions. As every part of life is an expression of myself, it's essential that these values are in unison with one another.

September 14

My passion drives me to succeed.

My love of goal-setting and wanting to help others push me to strive for greatness, knowing that if I am persistent in my effort, success will follow.

September 15

I need to lead.

Instead of being a mere spectator in my own life, I am determined to plot my own course. This way, I can live by the decisions that are solely mine and keep control over where this story takes me. There is no better feeling than carving out your path and determining what successes lay ahead. From today on, I'll be the one writing my stories.

September 16

I am allowed to disagree with others.

Everyone's opinion matters. I don't need to follow the majority just to fit in. My views are just as valid, so fearlessly asserting myself is both acceptable and necessary. Even when there may be disagreement with others, showing respect for differing opinions will allow me to proudly stand up for my beliefs.

September 17

I need to be honest with myself.

I won't whitewash anything or make excuses for my mistakes. I'm human and far from perfect, but that's alright because I am consistently expanding my knowledge and abilities. It is important to be truthful with myself about where I stand in life, while also pushing myself to get better each day.

September 18

I don't need to have all the answers.

Far from being intimidated by the thought of not knowing everything, I am instead moved to explore what lies outside my present realm of understanding. My approach is one that welcomes new possibilities and ideas in order to further enrich and expand my learning journey. Life should always be seen as an opportunity for exploration.

September 19

I am teachable.

I am open-minded and eager to soak up knowledge from all sources regardless of age, race, or background. I understand that each one of us has something valuable to offer and share with the world. With enthusiasm, I desire to learn as much as possible.

September 20

I am a good listener.

When I am engaged in a conversation, I make sure to listen intently and give my full attention to the speaker. This way, I can understand their words with clarity and provide meaningful feedback instead of simply awaiting my turn to speak.

September 21

I am insightful.

I am able to view things from several angles and present fresh viewpoints of my own. I am receptive to new ideas and am always eager to look at things differently. I am able to comprehend myself and the world around me better thanks to my insights.

September 22

I am nurturing.

My heart is full of kindness and compassion for those who are facing hardships in life. I'm always willing to be a source of strength by providing an understanding ear or a comforting embrace. With empathy as my foundation, my mission is to enhance the lives of those around me, helping one individual at a time.

September 23

I am able to imagine new things.

My creativity is one of my most powerful assets. I have the unique ability to envision what could be and bring it forth into reality. My dream-like state never stops as I continuously formulate new plans for an improved world.

September 24

I have the courage to be myself.

I am confident in who I am and am happy with myself. I don't have to put up a front or pretend to be someone else to please other people. I love and respect myself for who I am and accept myself for who I am.

September 25

I have the strength to keep going.

Though life is full of struggles, I persistently persevere. Overcoming adversity has made me stronger and more resilient, teaching me how to persist even in the face of insurmountable odds. My unwavering commitment propels me to accomplish my goals despite whatever obstacles block my path.

September 26

I am artistic.

I use creativity and art to express myself. I try to make work that makes other people happy because I see beauty in the world around me. I believe it is important to appreciate art because it is vital to living a full life.

September 27

I am innovative.

Constantly striving to become better, I enthusiastically embrace changes and relish taking risks. My out-of-the-ordinary thinking opens up opportunities for innovative solutions that others may never have considered before.

September 28

I am a lifelong learner.

I am a firm believer that learning should be an ongoing journey. I strive to fill my life with knowledge and new experiences so that I can reach greater heights both personally and professionally.

September 29

My dignity is intact.

I treat myself with dignity, honor, and respect at all times. Because I acknowledge my worthiness of love and admiration, whoever it may come from — no one's opinion can ever lower the value which I hold for myself.

September 30

I am a problem-solver.

I thrive on generating innovative solutions to problems. When posed with a difficult challenge, I will do whatever it takes to make the issue better and discover a viable answer. My creativity guarantees that no problem is too hard for me to overcome.

OCTOBER

October 1

I am in the right place doing the right thing.

This is my life. Despite enduring hardships, I continue to strive and persevere with a positive mentality while working diligently on improving myself. By doing so, I know that nothing can stop me from achieving success in any endeavor.

October 2

I intend to make my wishes come true.

I'll remain upbeat and strive to make the best of any situation. I understand that to some, this may seem audacious, but I want to accomplish my objectives while having fun. Life's too short to live with regrets.

October 3

I have a sharp mind.

I am a go-getter who loves to expand my knowledge and apply my quick wit to tackle obstacles that may seem insurmountable to others.

October 4

I have self-worth.

Although I have my strengths and weaknesses, nothing makes me feel more empowered than understanding the preciousness of my presence. I am neither feeble nor a timid soul; however, acknowledging and appreciating self-worth bring forth an incomparable sense of assurance in myself.

October 5

I have compassion.

"If you want others to be happy, practice compassion. If you want to be happy, practice compassion."

— Dalai Lama

October 6

I am trustworthy.

I pride myself on keeping my word, as I'm trustworthy and have no hidden motives. People recognize that what I say is true, which creates a bond of trust between us. Furthermore, it's not in my character to lie or exploit someone for personal gain.

October 7

I flow like a river.

My strength lies in my ability to be flexible, adjustable, and progressive. I'm open-minded and always evolving — never stuck in one place or another.

October 8

I am never in any danger.

I always feel safe as I am surrounded by compassionate people, and my guardian angels are in constant protection of me. Nothing is ever too difficult for me to handle, because I never have to go through anything alone.

October 9

My life is bursting with joy.

I'm so fortunate for the many blessings in my life. I have an encouraging family, genuine friends, and a home that provides me with peace of mind. My physical health is robust, as well as my mental state which brings me ample happiness and satisfaction throughout the day. Everywhere I go, smiling comes naturally, knowing how content I am in this moment — something to be extremely grateful for.

October 10

I am an inspiration for others.

My successes, regardless of size, encourage those around me to reach their own remarkable heights. I am a leader in my community, and my optimistic energy is infectious. When people witness my triumphs, they are inspired to go after their dreams with vigor and determination.

October 11

No one can dim the light within me.

I have total control over myself, and nobody has the power to make me feel inadequate. I firmly trust my qualities and skills. It doesn't matter what anyone says or does — nothing will extinguish my brightness. I am remarkably strong, highly capable of achieving anything that comes across my path, and absolutely meriting respect from all those around me.

October 12

I am not a quitter.

I refuse to surrender in the face of adversity, as I am confident that anything is achievable with hard work and perseverance. My aspirations will never be forgotten or abandoned. Instead, they will be pursued until their fruition is realized.

October 13

Taking care of myself is important.

I always prioritize my needs, because I know that they are essential and deserve to be met. My well-being is valuable, and it's never necessary for me to apologize for taking care of myself first.

October 14

My existence cannot be ignored.

My being here makes a significant impact in this world. My existence is essential, and my words will not go unheard. I possess an awe-inspiring niche that no one can take away from me; henceforth, I vow never to let anyone muffle my voice.

October 15

I love who I am becoming.

Every day, I strive to better myself and become the person who I want to be. With each passing day, my progress is evident in both small and large ways as I am slowly growing into a version of myself that makes me proud. Gradually but surely, I am arriving closer to my ideal self with every stride taken forward.

October 16

I should focus on myself.

My own bliss needs to be my top priority. Trying endlessly to satisfy others will not bring me joy, but rather I must do what brings me contentment and satisfaction. It's alright — even beneficial — for me to put myself before anyone else sometimes.

October 17

I am a fast learner.

I have a keen ability to absorb knowledge rapidly and retain information with ease. This makes me successful at both school and in life.

October 18

I take care of my body.

Taking care of my body is paramount and should be a top priority. I must make sure to exercise regularly, nourish myself with healthy foods, and get enough restful sleep in order for me to feel good about myself and reach greater levels of success.

October 19

I am appreciated.

The people in my life continually demonstrate their appreciation for me through their words and actions, reaffirming my worth and elevating my self-confidence. It is truly a wonderful feeling that encourages me to keep striving for success.

October 20

I need to stay calm.

In times of distress, I need to step away and take a breath. Keeping my composure will allow me to reason through issues more rationally and make wiser choices.

October 21

When I'm feeling down, a hug can always make me feel better.

A hug is a powerful thing. It can instantly lift my mood when I feel low. This small gesture of love and warmth tells me that someone cares about me, boosting my morale in an instant. With just one embrace, the world suddenly appears brighter than before.

October 22

I am a caring person.

I find joy in lending a helping hand and strive to make other people's lives better. Knowing that my efforts are having a positive impact gives me an immense sense of satisfaction.

October 23

I will make the most of this day.

Today, I will embrace all the things that not only provide me joy but also bring lasting benefits. To ensure I make the most of this day and leave feeling fulfilled, my outlook must be optimistic as I take full advantage of everything it has to offer.

October 24

I can bring smiles to people's faces.

Nothing brings me more joy than eliciting a smile from someone else. Knowing that I can make someone's day brighter is my ultimate goal, and it gives me an amazing feeling when I succeed.

October 25

I am making a positive impact on the world.

No matter our age, we can still have a noteworthy impact on the world. Let us all make an effort - no act of kindness is too small to be disregarded. Each one of us has something unique and valuable to contribute.

October 26

I am a natural winner.

I stay driven and persistently reach my goals because I trust in myself and am confident that I can triumph at any venture I pursue.

October 27

There is no limit to what I can achieve.

I am determined to succeed in whatever I decide to pursue. My aspirations fuel my ambition and instill within me the never-ending drive to persevere through adversity. With complete dedication, there is no limit to what greatness I can accomplish.

October 28

I always strive to do better.

I am never satisfied with mediocrity. I am constantly striving for excellence. My dedication and determination will result in tremendous success.

October 29

I am determined and persistent.

When obstacles arise, I refuse to quit. Instead, I strive for success with a steadfast determination that will not be deterred. Anything is possible if you put your mind to it and never give up on reaching your dreams.

October 30

I can adapt to new situations.

My ability to roll with the punches and remain composed in new situations is unrivaled. I'm always highly adaptable. Any changes thrown my way are met with a calm composure that enables me to easily adjust without getting flustered.

October 31

I have a knack for solving problems in creative ways.

I'm never timid to explore fresh ideas, and this allows me to conceive solutions that have yet to develop in the minds of others.

NOVEMBER

November 1

My spirit is unbreakable.

I trust my strength and capabilities to make it through any circumstance. I have consistently conquered obstacles, learning from them in the process. There is no chance of me ever abandoning myself or ceasing to strive for what I desire.

November 2

I love spending time with myself.

I relish any moment I have to myself, and I never am short of activities when alone. Endowed with the ability to keep my own company, I can entertain myself effortlessly while cherishing silence and resting in autonomy.

November 3

I know right from wrong.

I have a solid moral compass, and always make ethical choices that are mindful of the needs of all involved. It's easy for me to recognize what is right or wrong in any situation.

November 4

I am able to beat the odds.

I am a person who wholeheartedly embraces difficult tasks, confident that I have the fortitude to face them head-on and succeed. My perseverance is one of my greatest assets, as it has been instrumental in achieving positive outcomes time and time again.

November 5

I am excellent.

> "Excellence is not a gift, but a skill that takes practice. We do not act rightly because we are excellent, in fact we achieve excellence by acting rightly."
>
> — Plato

November 6

I have a great personality.

I have a natural sense of humor and self-assurance, and I'm quick to make friends. People are naturally drawn in by my sunny disposition without any conscious effort on my part. Exploring uncharted territories while making new connections is something that brings me immense joy.

November 7

I can turn a bad situation around.

I'm a great believer in turning negatives into positives. No matter how dire any given situation may be, I always manage to make the best of it and look at the brighter side of life. This positive attitude has been an invaluable asset for me throughout my life and gives me something hopeful to anticipate each day.

November 8

I can be counted on.

I am dependable and can always be trusted to fulfill my promises. I'm someone who will always come through in a pinch, as evidenced by the faith that friends and family have placed in me time after time. They know they have an unwavering ally when they turn to me for help.

November 9

I make things happen.

My ambition is unstoppable. When I take on a task, no obstacle can hinder my progress; I will relentlessly push forward until it's accomplished. My unyielding commitment has been the key factor in my successes throughout life.

November 10

I can think on my feet.

I am astute, agile, and able to think on my feet. This allows me to quickly come up with creative solutions in demanding settings, enabling me to remain ahead of the competition.

November 11

I have a lot of integrity.

Despite any difficulties, I constantly prioritize doing what is right. My dedication to morality and integrity has been my compass — guiding me through life's decisions with strength and clarity every step of the way. This commitment to righteousness truly serves me best in the long run.

November 12

I can recognize my shortcomings.

I'm certainly not flawless, and I freely admit this. Still, I make it a priority to welcome feedback in order to reach my full potential and continually work on improving myself.

November 13

I am a spreader of good news.

With an eternal enthusiasm, I am constantly radiating positivity and joyfully sharing it with others. By taking note of the positive in every situation, people can become encouraged no matter what they may be going through. My hopefulness is evidently contagious — it never fails to make someone smile.

November 14

I am always moving forward.

I never remain idle. I always push my boundaries and evolve in order to succeed. By persistently moving towards progress, it enables me to reach new heights of success and achieve the goals that I've set for myself.

November 15

I am always ahead of the curve.

As a perpetual learner, I'm constantly striving for knowledge and keeping my skills sharp. My passion for learning new things makes me an ideal student, ready to take on any challenge you give me. With this mindset, I always feel ahead of the pack and remain motivated in whatever task is at hand.

November 16

I am resourceful.

I'm incredibly resourceful, and with that, I can always identify solutions to any issue. This allows me to stay on track towards my aspirations unencumbered by life's obstacles.

November 17

I am charismatic.

With an inherent aptitude for engaging with people, I have the uncanny ability to make a lasting impression. My natural charisma is one of my most prominent qualities, and it never fails me in any given situation. Conversing comes easy to me, so you can always count on me when charm and poise are essential elements.

November 18

I have a great sense of humor.

Bringing joy to others is my specialty. From making someone smile with a clever joke, to being the life of the party — I love adding lightheartedness into any atmosphere. My ability to make people laugh never fails in lifting their spirits and bringing cheer on even the darkest days.

November 19

I can put myself in other people's shoes.

Even though I may not always agree with others, I make an effort to see things from their perspective and comprehend how they're feeling. This allows me to be more compassionate and tolerant of different opinions than my own.

November 20

I control my destiny.

I am the only one who holds the power to direct my future. I alone dictate how my life will unfold, and I take charge in making it happen.

November 21

I trust myself to make the right decisions.

I firmly believe in my capacity to make prudent decisions. I trust myself to choose what is most advantageous for me, and I am fully confident that I can determine the best options for me.

November 22

My future is bright.

I anticipate my future with enthusiasm and positivity, believing that possibilities are boundless and exciting opportunities await me.

November 23

I deserve the good things.

I possess the right to experience joy and accomplish greatness. I deserve to be celebrated, and should take full advantage of all that life has to offer me.

November 24

I stay true to myself.

"Always stay true to yourself and never let what somebody says distract you from your goals."

— Michelle Obama

November 25

I don't need to please everyone.

I'm empowered to communicate "no" with confidence. I don't have to prioritize others' desires ahead of mine, or take part in activities that aren't my cup of tea. My voice carries weight and I can be self-assured when defending my wants and needs.

November 26

I was given this life for a reason.

I am certain that I was placed in this world to fulfill a specific purpose. The gifts, talents, and abilities bestowed upon me are extraordinary. I have something exceptional to share with the Universe.

November 27

The challenges life presents make me stronger.

Difficulties are not obstacles, but rather chances to develop and form new skills. Through overcoming the struggles I face, I become stronger and wiser every day.

November 28

I can be both assertive and compassionate with my words.

I can communicate confidently without being domineering and still not compromise my values. I am capable of expressing myself in a way that is strong yet empathetic — firm but gentle.

November 29

I am willing to try new things and step out of my comfort zone.

Fearless and eager to explore, I embrace the unknown. Testing new waters energizes me, while taking risks is an adventure I'm passionate about experiencing.

November 30

Just getting started is the key.

Taking that first step can be tough. But I've discovered it's the key to success — once I'm moving, everything else falls into place. All it takes is a little momentum, then the rest will take care of itself.

DECEMBER

December 1

I create my own success.

I refuse to sit back and let life just happen. I am the one who will determine what true success looks like, then actively pursue it with vigor.

December 2

I persevere even when things are tough.

I am a warrior. No matter what obstacles stand in my way, I power through with strength and perseverance. Whenever things become difficult, I never surrender — I stay focused on my goal and remain resolute until I'm successful.

December 3

I am unstoppable.

I am overflowing with enthusiasm and dynamism. I'm never deterred by difficulty or obstacles, relentlessly pushing onward and achieving success. My relentless drive makes me unstoppable.

December 4

I embrace my imperfections.

I wholly embrace my imperfections and recognize them as part of what makes me so special. No one else on the planet is exactly like me, and I celebrate that by loving myself unconditionally.

December 5

I enjoy being alive.

I am deeply appreciative of the blessing of being alive. I savor every moment and value all that life has to offer. I'm here, and ready to live a life filled with vibrancy and joy.

December 6

I am generous.

I'm passionate about utilizing my time, energy, and resources to benefit others. Even if it's just a small gesture, I take pleasure in knowing that I've made someone else happy by giving back.

December 7

I let go of negative thoughts and cultivate positive ones.

I opt to concentrate on all the uplifting thoughts and leave behind any pessimism that seeks to come in. I am swirling with optimism, serenity, and happiness.

December 8

I dream big.

I am determined to make my grand goals a reality — I have unwavering confidence that I can turn them into success.

December 9

Luck is on my side.

I welcome good luck, positive experiences, and success with open arms. I am confident in my abilities to manifest the life that I desire through being optimistic in all facets of my life.

December 10

I take care of myself.

To keep my body, soul, and mind in tip-top shape I make sure to consume nutritious meals, remain active on a regular basis, and get enough rest. It is essential for me to take care of myself so that I can be the best version of me.

December 11

My safety is more important to me than anything else.

My safety and well-being always come first, so I will make sure to never take unnecessary risks.

December 12

My words have a lasting impact on others.

I am mindful of my choice of words, understanding that they possess the potential to shape and manipulate others' perspectives. Therefore, I select them with intentionality and purpose towards a positive end.

December 13

I'm always accountable for my own actions.

I maintain ownership over my own decisions and refuse to resort to blaming others for issues that I can personally resolve. Ultimately, it is me in control of both my joy and success.

December 14

I have a lot to be thankful for.

I am so thankful for the amazing blessings I receive, both big and small. From having a place to call home, food on my table, and people who care about me — I'm forever appreciative of all that life has given me. Truly grateful!

December 15

I'm doing the best I can.

Even when the going gets rough, I'm doing all that I can to give my best effort. It may not be possible for me to do everything, but in spite of this fact — I am pushing myself and striving to reach my full potential.

December 16

I am a force to be reckoned with.

I have the capability to make things happen in my life and will fight for what I believe in. Don't underestimate me. People must understand that they cannot take advantage of me.

December 17

I have many strengths that are unique to me.

I am an extraordinary individual with special skills and gifts that make me one-of-a-kind. I am filled with the utmost confidence and trust in my power to realize any goal I determine for myself.

December 18

I prioritize what works and ditch the rest.

I unchain myself from any negativity, apprehension, and worry that has been preventing me from moving forward. I accept new possibilities with an open heart and am eager to embrace what lies ahead on my journey. I welcome changes both small and large as part of my growth process.

December 19

No matter what I am feeling, it is valid.

I am completely entitled to every emotion that I feel, and I do not need to be embarrassed by them. It is valid for me to have my own feelings. They are an integral part of who I am as a person.

December 20

I am a person of my word.

Integrity and truthfulness are at the core of who I am. Keeping my promises is something that I take seriously. People can count on me to stay true to my word and follow through on any obligation that I make.

December 21

I am all ears to others.

I offer a compassionate and understanding ear to those around me, listening not only with my ears but also through an open heart.

December 22

I build relationships based on trust and mutual respect.

Honesty and respect define my interactions, laying the groundwork for strong connections with those around me. My relationships are built on trust — a cornerstone of meaningful connection that I continually strive to deepen.

December 23

I communicate effectively.

I communicate my thoughts articulately and with conviction. I lend an ear, allowing me to completely comprehend the message of others. If any miscommunication arises, I strive to resolve it promptly and efficiently.

December 24

I give 110% to everything that I do.

I'm the kind of person who never stops striving for excellence. I give 110% to everything in my life, from school and work to my personal projects — I always aim to be the best version of myself possible.

December 25

The universe has my back.

I am cherished and guarded. The universe is consoling me in my endeavors to reach all of my targets, while I bask in the warmth of love and blissful radiance.

December 26

I can beat stress.

I am confident that I can confront any obstacle thrown my way. With a composed head and unwavering strength, nothing is too hard for me to tackle. No matter the odds stacked against me, I embrace adversity with confidence and poise.

December 27

I am the coolest person ever.

I carry an air of poise and confidence, yet remain humorous and laid-back. I am personally content with myself, embracing all that I am. Whenever presented with a good time, it's inevitable that fun will ensue.

December 28

I am a magnet for good vibes only.

I manifest only the best of what life has to offer. I attract success, love, and abundance like a magnet. My circle is filled with people who have positive vibes and bring out the best in me.

December 29

I am a gift to my parents.

I am eternally thankful for the life I have been gifted with, and I recognize that my parents are blessed to have me in their lives. The pride emanating from them only further confirms this privilege of being their child — a joyous honor that I will always cherish.

December 30

I celebrate my successes... big and small!

I don't take any accomplishment for granted, no matter how small. I celebrate each victory as it brings me closer to my ultimate objectives.

December 31

I am excited for the year ahead.

Filled with optimism and anticipation, I am prepared to take on whatever the future holds. Bring it on, world! I am ready for whatever life has in store for me.

Conclusion

By incorporating these powerful positive affirmations into your day-to-day life, you can build unshakeable self-confidence and maintain a healthy mindset as a teenager. Don't let anything limit you from reaching all of your goals. Trust in yourself and strive for success.

When you trust in your own capabilities, overcoming obstacles becomes far simpler. You will be able to nurture a positive outlook on life while also seeing yourself differently — with more self-respect and belief.

Confidently recognize that you can do great things. So, cultivate a belief in yourself, and take the initiative to manifest your dreams!

Leaving a Review

As a self-published author, I find it important not only to write great books but also provide my readers with the best value possible. Being an Indie writer means I don't have access to all the perks of a traditional publisher, such as a publicist to get the word out about my latest releases. That's where you come in. A little bit of your time can go a long way towards helping me spread the word and I would be most appreciative if you would consider posting your honest thoughts about this book on Amazon.

Your review remains one of the most valuable promotional tools available. Reviews are vital in helping new readers find books they will enjoy reading. So if you've enjoyed this book, please consider leaving an honest rating or review by going to this book's page on Amazon. Good ratings and reviews from readers can help me attract new readers who will also enjoy my writing.

Thank you for your support,

Grace

References

30 Best CHARLES B. HANDY Quotes of 43. (n.d.). The Cite Site. Retrieved October 10, 2022, from https://thecitesite.com/authors/charles-b-handy/

53 Keep Trying Quotes to Motivate You to Never Quit. (2022, May 5). YourFates. Retrieved October 19, 2022, from https://www.yourfates.com/keep-trying-quotes/

A quote from Days of Blood & Starlight. (n.d.). Retrieved October 11, 2022, from https://www.goodreads.com/quotes/672780-as-long-as-you-re-alive-there-s-always-a-chance-things

A quote by Molly Friedenfeld. (n.d.). Retrieved October 11, 2022, from https://www.goodreads.com/quotes/3937231-your-heart-is-where-your-inner-light-resides-it-is

A quote by Oscar Wilde. (n.d.). Retrieved October 16, 2022, from https://www.goodreads.com/quotes/19884-be-yourself-everyone-else-is-already-taken

A quote by Vernon Howard. (n.d.). Retrieved October 12, 2022, from https://www.goodreads.com/quotes/424452-always-walk-through-life-as-if-you-have-something-new

Barack Obama Quotes. (n.d.). BrainyQuote. Retrieved October 19, 2022, from https://www.brainyquote.com/quotes/barack_obama_168698

Borge, J. (2021, May 19). 40 Positive Affirmations to Add to Your Daily Rotation. Oprah Daily. Retrieved October 21, 2022, from https://www.oprahdaily.com/life/relationships-love/g25629970/positive-affirmations/?slide=21

Desautels, B. (2022, August 9). *"To be yourself in a world that is constantly trying to change you is the greatest accomplishment."* Ralph Waldo Emerson. Bob Desautels. Retrieved October 21, 2022, from https://www.bobdesautels.com/blog/2018/8/6/

Edberg, H. (2022, August 12). 61 Everything Will Be OK Quotes to Help You When You Are Struggling. The Positivity Blog. Retrieved October 18, 2022, from https://www.positivityblog.com/everything-will-be-ok-quotes/

Excellence Quotes. (n.d.). BrainyQuote. Retrieved October 17, 2022, from https://www.brainyquote.com/topics/excellence-quotes

Gloria Steinem Quotes. (n.d.). BrainyQuote. Retrieved October 12, 2022, from https://www.brainyquote.com/quotes/gloria_steinem_121278

Good News Network. (2019, October 28). *"Destiny is no matter of chance. It is a matter of choice. It is not a thing to be waited for, it is a thing to be achieved."* – William Jennings Bryan. Retrieved October 18, 2022, from https://www.goodnewsnetwork.org/william-jennings-bryan-quote-on-destiny/

Henry Wadsworth Longfellow Quotes. (n.d.). BrainyQuote. Retrieved October 23, 2022, from https://www.brainyquote.com/quotes/henry_wadsworth_longfello_151369

"Honesty is the fastest way to prevent a mistake from turning into a failure." —James Altucher. (n.d.). The Foundation for a Better Life. Retrieved October 12, 2022, from https://www.passiton.com/inspirational-quotes/7793-honesty-is-the-fastest-way-to-prevent-a-mistake

If you want others to be happy, practice compassion. If you want to be happy, practice compassion. (n.d.). The Random Acts of Kindness Foundation. Retrieved October 19, 2022, from https://www.randomactsofkindness.org/kindness-quotes/143-if-you-want-others-to

I'm better than I used to be. Better than I was yesterday. (n.d.). IdleHearts. Retrieved October 19, 2022, from https://www.idlehearts.com/2081712/im-better-than-i-used-to-be-better-than-i-was-yesterday

Krissy Cela. (n.d.). Retrieved October 11, 2022, from https://www.krissycela.com/blog-posts/self-love-lessons-from-our-ambassadors

Lindsay Fox Quotes. (n.d.). BrainyQuote. Retrieved October 23, 2022, from https://www.brainyquote.com/quotes/lindsay_fox_546094

Meah, A. (2017, July 6). 30 Inspirational Quotes On Excellence. AwakenTheGreatnessWithin. Retrieved October 17, 2022, from https://www.awakenthegreatnesswithin.com/30-inspirational-quotes-on-excellence/

Our greatest glory is not in never failing, but in rising every time w...-Confucius | Confucius Quotes. (n.d.). Quotss. Retrieved October 13, 2022, from http://www.quotss.com/quote/Our-greatest-glory-is-not-in-never-failing-but-in-rising-every-time-we-fai

quotespedia.org. (2020, October 21). Always be a first rate version of yourself and not a second rate... Quotespedia.org. Retrieved October 23, 2022, from https://www.quotespedia.org/authors/j/judy-garland/always-be-a-first-rate-version-of-yourself-and-not-a-second-rate-version-of-someone-else-judy-garland/

Ralph Waldo Emerson Quotes. (n.d.). BrainyQuote. Retrieved October 23, 2022, from https://www.brainyquote.com/quotes/ralph_waldo_emerson_387459

Sasson, R. (2020, January 22). *Abundance Quotes and Sayings to Enrich Your Life.* Success Consciousness | Positive Thinking - Personal Development. Retrieved October 15, 2022, from https://www.successconsciousness.com/blog/quotes/abundance-quotes/

Say, J. (2020, October 9). 43 Inspirational Charlie Chaplin Quotes (BEST). Gracious Quotes. Retrieved October 16, 2022, from https://graciousquotes.com/charlie-chaplin/

Timothy Weah Quotes. (n.d.). BrainyQuote. Retrieved October 15, 2022, from https://www.brainyquote.com/quotes/timothy_weah_975475

William Jennings Bryan Quotes. (n.d.). BrainyQuote. Retrieved October 18, 2022, from https://www.brainyquote.com/quotes/william_jennings_bryan_389006

Yadav, S. (2017, July 25). 21 Quotes That Will Inspire You to Create Your Destiny. Pick the Brain | Motivation and Self Improvement. Retrieved October 19, 2022, from https://www.pickthebrain.com/blog/21-quotes-that-will-inspire-you-to-create-your-destiny/

About the Author

Grace is a well-known parenting author who has written several books on the topic. She has dedicated her life to assisting families through her writings. Her greatest enjoyment in life is being a mother because it's the most gratifying job she's ever had. She likes to write books that touch on all the different aspects of parenting and personal experiences, such as her encounters with her children.

Her love for writing began when she discovered a parenting technique for her explosive son, who was diagnosed with ADHD and ODD, that outperformed others. She was determined to get the word out to other parents as soon as possible. With time, this has developed into something bigger where she is able to share great pieces of advice that can truly change lives.

She also incorporates insights from other parents to offer an enlightening reading experience for all of her readers. Grace hopes that families will be inspired to change the way they think and make better parenting decisions by reading her books.

She enjoys reading novels and watching movies with her family on the weekends.

Visit her profile on Amazon to learn more about her other works - **https://www.amazon.com/author/gracecohen**